The Best
BABY
SHOWER
BOOK

A Complete Guide for Party Planners

COURTNEY COOKE

Meadowbrook Press

Distributed by Simon & Schuster
New York

Library of Congress Cataloging-in-Publication Data
Cooke, Courtney.
    The best baby shower book: a complete guide for party planners / Courtney Cooke.—Rev.
        p.   cm.
    ISBN 978-0-88166-384-6 (Meadowbrook)—ISBN 978-0-7432-1243-4 (Simon &
    Schuster)
        1. Showers (Parties) I. Title.

    GV1472.7.S5 C66 2001
    793.2—dc21   00-051132

Editorial Director: Christine Zuchora-Walske
Contributing Editor: Becky Long
Copyeditors: Kathleen Martin-James, Megan McGinnis
Proofreader: Angela Wiechmann
Production Manager: Paul Woods
Graphic Design Manager: Tamara Peterson
Illustrations: Joyce Shelton, Terri Moll

Published by Meadowbrook Press
            6110 Blue Circle Drive, Suite 237
            Minnetonka, MN 55343
www.meadowbrookpress.com

BOOK TRADE DISTRIBUTION by Simon & Schuster, a division of Simon and Schuster,
Inc., 1230 Avenue of the Americas, New York, NY 10020

16 15 14 13 12   12 11 10 9 8 7 6

Printed in the United States of America

Acknowledgments

We would like to thank all of the people who answered our questionnaires and, in particular, the following people, without whose input the book would not have been complete:

Diane Camp, Lori Carleton, Carol Cook, Dorothy Cook, Mary Curran, Barbara DeGroot, Colleen Finochiaro, Elaine Fong, Elizabeth Foyt, Karen Hamilton, Shannon Jahnke, Betty Lundquist, Lynn Miller, Minnetonka Lutheran Nursery School, Dorothy Stuber, and Barbara Unell.

Contents

Buying the Gifts

Appendix

Introduction

Your best friend calls with fantastic news. She's pregnant! There are many details to discuss and, in the heat of the moment, you say you'd love to throw her a baby shower. Then you hang up the phone—and panic sets in. You hate showers with their dumb games and endless small talk. You imagine your reputation for throwing great parties being destroyed. You, however, are stuck. You're the logical person to give the shower, and it's too late to back out. You ask yourself if it's possible to turn a tired old shower into a great party. You bet it is!

When you think about it, it's probably the trappings of the traditional baby shower that you dislike: silly games, fussy decorations, and fattening foods. In *The Best Baby Shower Book,* you'll find tips to help you plan a fun, contemporary celebration that suits you, your guests, and the expectant mom (and dad, if he's included). We've created a practical handbook that includes time- and money-saving hints for decorations and food. It contains innovative gift ideas and exciting alternatives to outdated games. We also suggest including men in the celebration—they're expectant parents, too!

A baby shower is, above all, a celebration of the couple's decision to have a baby. The party combines needed gifts for the expectant parents with good wishes and good advice. So don't hesitate to throw a baby shower—just forget those stodgy old showers you shudder to remember, pack away your panic, dust off your "great party" reputation (or plan to start one), and read on. You're about to throw one heck of a party!

Planning a Shower

In addition to celebrating a new life, a baby shower helps expectant parents acquire baby-related items that may otherwise drain the family's bank account. The party also provides emotional support for the mom-to-be who may be anxious about taking on her new role as parent. Plan your celebration so that these objectives will be met.

Keep in mind, too, that the dad-to-be may also need some emotional support and would welcome the good wishes and good advice a shower offers. Showers for the expectant couple are gaining popularity, and the key to planning one is to plan it as if it were a regular get-together. A couple's shower will be most relaxed if both the male and female guests know one another fairly well. Gag gifts, "fatherly" and "motherly" advice, and the company of friends can be all it takes for this kind of shower to be a success.

For simplicity's sake, we've written most of the shower themes and activities with the mom-to-be in mind. But know that you can modify any of the themes and activities to fit a couple's shower.

Setting the Date

The first thing you should do as host is set a date and time for the shower. Begin by asking the expectant mom (and dad, if he's included) at least two to three months before the baby's due date about available dates. Because her schedule will likely be hectic in the weeks prior to and right after the baby's birth, ask her whether she'd prefer a shower before or after the baby's born. Both times have advantages. Parents expecting their first child may need the baby-related items they'd receive at a shower held three to six weeks before the birth. And because the last weeks of pregnancy can be trying, a prebaby shower can give the mom-to-be valuable emotional support.

If the mom-to-be prefers a shower after the baby's birth, you'll have the advantage of knowing the baby's sex (which some parents still choose not to learn or make public before the baby arrives). Guests can then buy or make sex-specific gifts. Of course, this shower also sets the stage for an appearance by the real guest of honor—the baby!

Anticipate potential scheduling problems for your guests, particularly if your list includes people traveling long distances. Try to find a date and time that accommodates everyone.

Don't forget to check the calendar for major holidays or cultural events that may conflict with your shower date, such as Memorial Day weekend or the Super Bowl.

The Guest List

Prepare your guest list by talking to the mom-to-be first. She'll know who should or should not be invited. If you're planning a surprise shower, the couple's parents or close friends will be happy to furnish you with a list of names, addresses, and phone numbers. Ask for this information well ahead of time.

If you know the mom-to-be through a club or organization, if you work with her, or if you have a group of mutual friends, you may already have a ready-made guest list, one in which the guests know one another. Nevertheless, always consult with the mom-to-be before finalizing the list.

Choosing a Location

The location and availability of a given venue will influence your shower date and guest list, so think about the where well in advance. Also consider that while your home may be a convenient and inexpensive shower site for you, the location may be inconvenient for many of your guests, who may be forced to travel far. If that's the case, consider a more central location.

While restaurants and clubs are obvious party spots, don't hesitate to try someplace different, such as a day spa, bed-and-breakfast, and so on. Try to find a place that will create the right ambiance for your celebration or that offers an activity your guests will enjoy.

Invitations

Depending upon the style of the shower and the size of the guest list, you can either send written invitations or invite people by phone. A written invitation insures that important party details are communicated cor-rectly. It also serves as a nice keepsake for the baby's scrapbook. (For tips on making your own invitations, see page 80.)

Be sure to include the following items on written invitations: the date, time, and address (including directions) of the party; the name(s) of the expectant parent(s); your name, address, and phone number; gift registry information; theme information; and RSVP information. If you ask guests to RSVP, they're expected to notify you whether they'll be attending. If you write "Regrets only," guests are expected to respond only if they won't be attending. You should also give a deadline for the response. To get a good response, mail the invitations at least three weeks before the shower date.

Celebrating Every Baby

Remember, baby showers aren't just for celebrating first babies. Every baby deserves a special welcome. Besides, it's likely that the more children expec-tant parents have, the more they will appreciate baby-related gifts.

Dos and Don'ts

- **Do** plan ahead. Send your invitations at least three weeks before the shower.
- **Do** get organized before the shower so the party will run smoothly. This way, you'll have time to actually enjoy the shower.
- **Do** consider including men.
- **Do** have fun with decorations. Consider using decorations or centerpieces that incorporate baby-related items, which can be given to the mom-to-be at the end of the party.
- **Do** include a bunch of balloons outside your door to greet guests.
- **Do** use your best linens and silver if you're planning a formal party.
- **Do** present foods attractively. Include garnishes.
- **Do** know your guests' dietary restrictions when planning the menu, especially those of the mom-to-be. If you plan to serve alcoholic beverages, label them clearly.
- **Do** serve foods that are easy to eat.
- **Don't** expect guests to balance a sit-down meal on their laps.
- **Do** seat one or two detail-minded persons near the mom-to-be to handle gift-wrapping and record the gifts.
- **Don't** give all newborn or three-month-size clothing. The baby will soon wear larger sizes.
- **Do** remember both expectant parents when buying gifts. Personal gifts can give them a real lift during this stressful time.
- **Do** consider using the nursery colors in your decorations.
- **Do** keep the shower short and sweet (usually two to three hours).
- **Do** plan activities that guests will enjoy.
- **Don't** play games that are embarrassing or awkward.
- **Do** select useful prizes for guests.
- Finally, **do** have a good time!

5

Checklist

A checklist can be useful when planning your shower. Checking off completed tasks allows you to concentrate on other details. Also, post your menu in a handy spot. The reminder will help you prepare your shopping list. It'll also help remind you to borrow those three serving dishes, two card tables, and a punch bowl!

Two to Three Months before the Baby's Due Date

- ❑ Consult with the expectant mom (and dad, if necessary) and select a date and time for the shower.
- ❑ Prepare a guest list.
- ❑ Choose a location and secure a venue.

One Month before the Shower

- ❑ Decide on a theme (optional).
- ❑ Make or buy invitations.

Three Weeks before the Shower

- ❑ Check the required postage for invitations.
- ❑ Have someone proofread the invitations for missing details or typos.
- ❑ Mail the invitations.
- ❑ Plan the menu.
- ❑ Plan the activities and prizes.
- ❑ Decide on your gift. (Allow more time if you plan to make your gift.)

One to Two Weeks before the Shower
❑ Make or buy decorations.
❑ Buy or complete your gift. (Wrap it now and avoid the last-minute rush!)
❑ Prepare your shopping list for menu ingredients.

One Week before the Shower
❑ Check that all appropriate serving dishes and utensils are on hand.
❑ Check that enough tables and chairs are on hand and in good repair.
❑ Wash and iron table linens, if necessary.
❑ Check RSVPs to determine the number of guests.
❑ Call the mom-to-be to remind her of the shower.

Three Days before the Shower
❑ Buy all groceries except fresh bread and rolls.
❑ Order centerpiece and other fresh flowers, if necessary.
❑ Clean the house.
❑ Check that all appropriate serving dishes and utensils are clean.
❑ Buy film, tapes, and batteries for camera and video camera.
❑ Prepare nametags and place cards.

The Day before the Shower
❑ Prepare as much of the menu as possible.
❑ Set the table and decorate the party room.
❑ Bring tables and chairs out of storage. Set up if possible.
❑ Assemble items that will be used for activities.
❑ Wrap the prizes (and your gift, if you haven't already done so).

The Day of the Shower

❑ Arrange your centerpiece or pick it up at the flower shop.
❑ Buy fresh bread and rolls.
❑ Finish last-minute dusting and vacuuming.
❑ Set out coasters.
❑ Prepare the rest of the menu.
❑ Have a pen and paper ready for someone to record the gifts. (See the Shower Gift Record on page 90.)
❑ Set out a box and paper bag to store gifts and gift-wrapping.

Last-Minute Details

❑ Don't be surprised by an early arrival! Get dressed at least thirty minutes to an hour before guests are expected to arrive.

❑ Have coffee ready to brew and other beverages ready to serve.
❑ Greet guests and have a good time!

Choosing a Theme

Incorporating a theme in your shower is optional, but it may help you coordinate the various aspects of your party. A theme can also make gift hunting easier for guests. If you know the mom-to-be will be enjoying several showers, you may want to narrow the scope of your party to provide her with gifts she won't receive elsewhere.

Simple themes often work best, such as ones centered on a traditional symbol of a newborn. (See Baby Shower Clip Art on page 81 for inspiration.) We've outlined several themes in the following pages, including creative suggestions for invitations, decorations, gift ideas, activities, and food. Remember, you don't have to spend a lot of money. The best party details may be those you make yourself. As you read on, consider how certain ideas might work independently of any particular theme, or mix and match various ideas to create your own theme.

Diaper Shower

Diapers are the quintessential baby fashion accessory, so why not make them the focus of your party?

Invitations
Write party details on a sheet of stationery. Fold it to resemble a trifold diaper and fasten it with a gold safety pin. (See illustration on page 82.) Or fold and fasten a piece of white or pastel flannel. Write party details on a cardstock postcard and insert it into the cloth diaper.

Decorations
For a centerpiece, diaper a potted plant or vase of flowers with a piece of baby-themed fabric. Secure the fabric with diaper pins. Give the centerpiece to the mom-to-be after the party. Also, see the illustration on page 82 to fold napkins. Stuff silverware into folded diaper napkins.

Gift Ideas
Give a diaper cake. To make one, open one disposable diaper and roll it up. Open a second diaper and wrap it around the first. Continue rolling diapers to form even layers. Secure the finished "cake" with tape and curling ribbon. Decorate with baby essentials such as pacifiers or stuffed toys. Roll other small gifts between the diapers if you wish.

Special Touches
For nametags, cut out triangles from pink and blue paper and fold each into a diaper. (See illustration on page 82.) Upon their arrival, have guests write their names on the diapers. Fasten each with a gold safety pin. Award prizes to guests who picked the "dirty" diapers (tags dabbed with mustard inside).

Teddy Bear Shower

Nothing is as cuddly as a new baby or a teddy bear. Combine the two for a shower that will leave guests feeling warm and fuzzy.

Invitations

Use the bear template on page 83 to design a gift card. Write party details on it and attach it to a small stuffed bear. Hand-deliver or mail each bear invitation. If mailing the invitation, cut "air holes" in the box and label it with a phrase like "Please don't feed the bear."

Decorations

Invite guests to bring a favorite teddy bear. Use them as decorations. As an icebreaker, have each guest tell a story about his or her bear. Award prizes for the funniest bear names or stories.

Gift Ideas

Challenge guests to give gifts that either are bare essentials or are bear-related, such as a sleeper with a bear motif, teddy bear for the baby, or a sexy teddy for the mom-to-be.

Special Touches

Check out local craft stores that offer teddy bear workshops in which guests can make custom-designed bears for the baby. Make bear-shaped nametags. (See the template on page 83.)

Family Tree Shower

This shower is a great way to celebrate the budding of a new branch on the family tree.

Invitations
Design family trees on cardstock. Write party details on the leaves. (See the template on page 84.)

Decorations
For a centerpiece, create a family tree by sticking branches from an ornamental or flowering tree in a vase weighted with sand or marbles. Hang baby-related items, such as rattles, toys, or booties, from the branches. Or if the guests are primarily relatives, hang a small, framed baby photo of each from the tree, using pink and blue ribbons. Challenge guests to identify the babies. Give the tree to the mom-to-be after the party.

Gift Ideas
As a group gift, give a gift certificate to a tree nursery, where the expectant parents can find the perfect tree to plant in their baby's honor.

Special Touches
Write guests' names on large leaves made of silk and use them as nametags or place cards. Or use the leaf template on page 84. Give guests seedlings as favors.

Hang family photos on a wall for a caption contest. Upon arrival, assign each guest a photo and have him or her write a caption for it. Award prizes for the funniest contributions. Place the photos and captions in an album for the mom-to-be. Or show childhood videos of the expectant parents.

Shower for the Little Cowboy or Cowgirl

This shower is especially fun for both expectant parents. Invite guests to wear cowboy hats, boots, and jeans. Hold the shower, complete with barbecue, in your yard.

Invitations

Write party details on a gift card and tie it to a toy cowboy hat. Or wrap the card in a bandanna that the guest can wear to the shower. Or make a cowboy hat invitation using the template on page 85.

Include a "Most Wanted" list that features gift ideas. To make the list look old, rub a teabag all over it and add a few "bullet holes" by punching a pencil through the paper and coloring around the holes with charcoal.

Decorations

Hang signs that read "Welcome to Ranch Baby." Design a "brand" using the baby's initials (if you know what they are). Feature the personalized brand in your decorations.

Gift Ideas

For a group gift, buy a rocking horse. Or follow this Texas custom: Have guests fill a piggy bank with money for the expectant parents.

Special Touches

For nametags, write names on toy sheriff badges.

Shower for Multiples

For the couple expecting more than one baby, a shower that provides items in multiples will always be welcome.

Invitations

Make a paper chain invitation that features the anticipated number of babies. (See illustration on page 86.)

Decorations

Have the same number of centerpieces as there are expected babies. If you know the babies' sexes, arrange the centerpieces in corresponding colors. Decorate with baby paper chains. (See illustration on page 86.)

Gift Ideas

Many parents of multiples struggle just to provide the basics for their children. The following are items that these parents need most. Keep in mind that some parents of multiples may appreciate "frivolous" gifts for their little ones even more than practical ones.

Equipment

Pool funds to buy an expensive item, such as an extra car seat, swing, crib, highchair, or play equipment for the yard. A stroller designed for multiples is also an ideal gift. (Note: Side-by-side strollers don't fit through doorways easily.) Remember that this equipment will receive multiple use, so quality and durability are extra important.

Clothing

Every piece of baby clothing (including shoes) will be needed in multiples. Ask the expectant parents how they feel about dressing the babies alike. Some wouldn't dream of it, while others can't wait. Share their feelings with guests.

Magazine Subscription

A subscription to a magazine about parenting multiples, such as *TWINS Magazine,* is especially useful to expectant parents before the babies are born—they'll actually have time to read! (Find out how to order on page 77.)

Other Ideas

Give a keepsake book the expectant parents can use to track the babies' schedules (who eats first, who naps longer, and so on) and preferences. The book will also help caregivers stay organized.

Special Touches

Offers of help will be greatly appreciated by overworked parents of multiples. Consider giving gift certificates to help with meals, baby-sitting, or even driving. (It's hard enough to load one baby into the car for a doctor's appointment, let alone two or more!)

Block Shower

While this shower can stand on its own, if you and the mom-to-be live in a close-knit neighborhood, it's also a twist on a block party. Plus, it's an ideal way to include men and entire families in the celebration. Make it a surprise shower. Notify everyone but the guest of honor that the party is really a baby shower. Of course, make sure the mom-to-be can attend the "block party"!

Invitations

Write party details on a plain block of wood. Or glue paper cutouts featuring party details on all sides of a toy block.

Decorations

Ask guests to wrap their gifts to look like blocks. Use packages of disposable diapers as decorative building blocks.

Gift Ideas

As a group project, make a block mirror for the baby's nursery. Glue alphabet blocks around a 12-inch-square mirror using a glue that adheres to glass. Consider arranging the blocks to spell out the baby's name. Glue hardware onto the back of the mirror for hanging.

Special Touches

Using frosting, design toy blocks to spell out "congratulations" on a sheet cake.

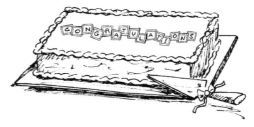

Office Shower

An office party is fun if coworkers are close and enjoy one another's company. It's also one you can easily plan as a surprise. Schedule a convenient time and place for the shower—perhaps a long lunch in a restaurant near work or in the company break room. Or consider a get-together at your home, if guests don't have to travel too far.

Invitations
If you're inviting many guests, design the invitation to look like an office memo. For a more intimate group, design the invitation to look like a message slip and deliver it personally.

Decorations
Have coworkers bring baby photos of themselves to the party. Tape the photos to the wall and challenge guests to identify who's who. Have them write captions for the photos. Award a prize to the guest who identifies the most babies and another to the guest who comes up with the funniest caption.

Gift Ideas
Pool funds and present a group monetary gift.

Special Touches
Lighten the expectant mom's workload when she returns from maternity leave. Give her gift certificates for various work-related tasks to be completed by coworkers. Or give her plenty of film and frames so she can display baby photos in her office.

Pink-or-Blue Shower

This shower is ideal if you know the baby's sex.

Invitations
Use pink or blue invitations.

Decorations
Fill the room with either pink or blue balloons and have centerpieces arranged in the appropriate color. Invite guests to come dressed in either pink or blue.

Gift Ideas
Anything and everything in pink or blue is perfect. Make a corsage for the mom-to-be from fancy baby socks, ribbons, and silk flowers in the appropriate color. Send guests home with pink or blue candies wrapped in corresponding tulle.

Special Touches
Serve refreshments that are either pink or blue. Have a bakery lightly tint bread pink or blue for finger sandwiches. Other menu options include blueberry cheesecake, frozen strawberry drinks, and nachos made with blue corn chips. Or make the meal a potluck and challenge guests to bring dishes that are either pink or blue.

Baby Quilt Shower

This party will provide a personalized keepsake that will last a lifetime.

Invitations

Cut out squares from a fabric whose color coordinates with the nursery.
Send a square to each guest with a note featuring the party details and an
invitation for each to embroider, paint, or appliqué a design onto the fabric.
Ask guests to initial the squares.

Decorations

Use old quilts as tablecloths. Cut out place mats from calico fabric.
Use coordinating paper napkins in a patchwork design.

Gift Ideas

Ask guests to send you their squares ahead of time so the quilt can be
assembled and then be given at the shower. Or have guests bring their
squares to the shower, and you assemble the quilt at a later date. Another
idea is to have guests sign the back of a finished quilt with permanent
markers. Embroider the signatures later, if you wish.

Special Touches

Design the quilt using fabric scraps from the mom- and dad-to-be's favorite
childhood clothing. Transfer photos of mom- or dad-to-be wearing the
garments onto the finished quilt. (To make a photo transfer, take the photo
to a copy center and have it transferred onto iron-on paper. Then iron the
design onto the fabric.)

Time-of-Day Shower

When the baby arrives, new parents will spend the hours in a day doing things that are very different from what they're used to. This shower has fun with that imminent chaos. You assign each guest an hour in a typical day in the new parents' lives, and guests bring corresponding gifts. The result will be a booty of useful baby items.

Invitations

Write party details on a gift card attached to a toy watch. Assign a different time of day to each guest and ask that he or she brings a corresponding gift. You could also provide gift suggestions for each assigned time. For example, an appropriate gift for an 8:00 P.M. assignment could be bedtime goodies, such as books, blankets, or sleepers.

Decorations

Draw a clock face on a tablecloth. Use toy watches as napkin rings.

Gift Ideas

Ask each guest to introduce the opening of his or her gift with a clever story about what might occur at that hour on a typical day. For example, here's an introduction that could be read before the 3:00 A.M. gift is opened: "It's 3:00 A.M. and [parents' names] wake to the sound of their new alarm clock. Unfortunately, there's no snooze button on this state-of-the-art gadget, but it does feature a good set of lungs. Let's see if there's something that Baby [baby's last name] might need...." The 3:00 A.M. present, which could be a music box that plays a lullaby, is then opened. Consider videotaping the gift opening or asking guests to write their stories on gift cards as keepsakes.

Special Touches

Send guests home with bath time or bedtime goodies, such as bubble bath or tea.

Keeping the Party Rolling

Your guests are arriving this afternoon at three, and suddenly you wonder: What will we do? Should you plan some activities (Warning! Stodgy old shower alert!) or leave guests free to entertain themselves?

Activities can be crucial to maintaining a high level of fun. If your guests aren't well acquainted, playing an icebreaker game can get people talking. If guests know one another well but haven't visited in a long time, you might limit game-playing time so guests can chat. Whatever you choose to do, remember to carefully match the activities with your guests' personalities. Well-planned party activities avoid a few common pitfalls, so keep in mind the following questions while you're brainstorming ideas:

- Will the activity encourage conversation? (Requiring guests to write answers to questions can, in some situations, suppress conversation. Also, writing answers while balancing cake and punch on your lap can be tricky.)
- Will the activities embarrass any of my guests?

✤ Are the games really fun? (To find out, ask yourself if you'd enjoy playing them at a nonshower party, or talk to someone who's already tried the game.)

The following activities answer these questions and virtually guarantee that your party will be a smashing success.

Icebreakers

Best Wishes

Set a guest book on the table with the nametags.
Display a card near it that asks guests to sign their names and write best wishes and/or advice for the mom-to-be.

The Baby Profile

Have guests help you predict the expected baby's attributes, but don't let them know they're doing so! As each guest arrives, choose a category from the Baby Profile Form on page 92 and ask him or her to give you an appropriate word to fill in the blank. Guests unknowingly choose the baby's sex, first name, middle name, hair color, eye color, and so on. For the height blank, limit the possibilities to numbers between fifty-four and eighty-four. Limit the weight options to numbers between ninety-five and three hundred. Add more categories, if necessary, so that each guest provides one attribute. When the baby's profile is complete, guests will enjoy hearing that the baby will become a "female plumber who has green hair and orange eyes, is six feet tall, weighs ninety-five pounds, and eats chopped liver." Give the mom-to-be the profile as a keepsake.

Advice

To make introductions interesting, have each guest relate his or her favorite (serious or funny) piece of parenting advice. Record this sage wisdom along with the names of the advisers in a notebook for the mom-to-be. Or videotape the advice session. If the guests all know each other, just eliminate the introductions and the activity is still fun. And, of course, don't pressure anyone to join in. Some guests will be more eager to give advice than others will.

Guess the Nametags

Prepare nametags in advance. Draw a small baby-related item on each tag. Without letting them see the nametags, attach guests' nametags to their backs. (Remember to cover your mirrors!) Have guests ask one another yes-or-no questions to figure out the items on their own backs. This activity helps guests who don't know each other learn one another's names. Award a prize to the first (and perhaps last) person to guess his or her item.

Guess the Beans

Pour pink and blue jellybeans into a fancy transparent baby bottle, such as one that's been hand-painted or molded into a fun shape. Set the bottle on the table near the entrance. Beside it, set out pencils and slips of paper. As guests arrive, have them guess the number of beans in the bottle, then have them drop the slips into a bowl. Award a prize to the guest who guesses closest to the correct number of beans. Make sure you've counted the beans before the party, of course!

Fun-for-All Games and Activities

How My Baby Changed My Life

Ask guests to bring a written story relating their own frustrating, joyful, or humorous parenting experiences. Collect the stories in a homemade book. If you want to use a particular type of paper in the book, send a sheet to each guest before the party. Or simply ask guests to use a specific kind of paper. Make and decorate a book cover in advance. Punch holes along the sides of the pages and cover and string them together with ribbon. Or insert the pages into a three-ring binder. Ask guests to read aloud their stories at the party. (Warn them about this activity ahead of time!)

Lights, Camera, Action

Have someone videotape the shower. In years to come, the child and parents will love watching this treasured momento.

Instant Replay

If you have an instant camera, take snapshots throughout the shower. Include shots of each guest, the buffet or dinner table before eating, and the mom-to-be as she opens each gift. Insert the photos into an album. Don't worry if you have blank album pages left over; the parents can use them for photos of their baby's first year.

Embroidery Party

If your guest list comprises people who love to sew, distribute a cloth diaper to each guest and provide embroidery needles and thread. Ask guests to stitch a design, such as flowers or hearts, on the seat of the diapers. This activity is great for boosting conversation while everyone works, and the results can be used either as diapers or burping pads.

Name the Baby Food

Select several different jars of baby food and number each jar. Remove the labels and have guests guess the contents of each jar and give it a fun name. (Be sure to provide paper and pencils.) Award a prize to the guest who correctly identifies the most baby food and another to the guest who comes up with the most creative baby food names.

Who's the Baby?

Ask guests to bring baby photos of themselves. Collect the photos and stash them until everyone arrives. (This way, the earlier guests don't have an advantage over later arrivals.) Give each guest a copy of the guest list with a blank next to each name. Number the photos and display them in an album. Have guests fill out their forms, guessing who's who. The guest who correctly identifies the most photos wins a prize. When guests have reclaimed their photos, give the album to the mom-to-be.

This Is Your Life

This activity is patterned after the old TV show and is perfect if your guests are family members or old friends. First, prepare a short slide show of the expectant mom as a child. Or show family movies of her. Have guests predict the baby's attributes by seeing his or her parent as a kid. Next, include a "mystery guest." Choose someone who knew the mom-to-be way back when. Have the mystery guest hide behind a curtain while he or she shares some stories about the guest of honor. Then ask the mom-to-be to guess who's talking about her. This activity is especially fun if you can include someone unexpected and welcome as the mystery guest.

Sure-Fire Sex Determination

This activity is far from scientific, but it's lots of fun. To guess the sex of the baby, turn to page 87 for a series of sex-determining questions and tests based on folklore. Use the form to record the results. Give the form as a keepsake for the mom-to-be. After the baby is born, you can decide which prediction methods are most accurate.

Roast

This activity is perfect for a couple's shower. Ask guests to take turns telling stories about the baby's parents, applying them to the way the baby will be. Encourage humorous yet friendly, outrageous yet tasteful recollections. The longer guests have known the parents, the funnier this activity will be.

Baby Pool

This activity is especially fun if your guests enjoy betting. Copy the Baby Pool Forms on page 88. Give each guest a copy and have him or her guess the baby's birth date, time of birth, sex, length, and weight.

Everyone will try harder if you offer a prize, so advertise one. Take up a collection, a dollar per entry. Allow guests to enter as many times as they wish. Half of the collection will go to a savings account for the baby and half will go to the winner of the bet.

Of course, guests will have to wait until the baby's birth to find out who wins the bet. To score, award three points each to the guests who came closest to correctly guessing the birth date, time of birth, length, and weight; award two points each to guests who came second closest, and one point each to guests who came third closest. Award two points to each guest who guessed the sex correctly. The guest with the most points wins the pool.

Unstructured Activities

Who says baby showers must have structured activities? If your guests know one other well, provide ample food, comfortable surroundings, some music, and let them mix and mingle.

If you want to bring guests together, introduce one of the conversation starters on the next page. These topics can help get a conversation rolling. Use them as a structured activity or sneak them in casually. Toss out these topics to the whole group or ask the views of one guest at a time.

- The way times have changed, especially regarding child rearing (The discussion could include discipline, developmental theories, baby equipment, doctors, and so on.)
- The funniest thing your baby has ever done
- The most frustrating part of being a new parent
- The best or worst advice for a new parent
- The best or worst experience you had as a parent
- The best or worst experience you had growing up

Prizes

The best prizes are those that are fun and useful. Spend a little more money on a few nice prizes rather than buy a lot of cheap, useless ones. Keep your guest list in mind when choosing the prizes, and remember that tastes can vary dramatically. Since you have no idea who will win which prize, stick with universally well-received items. And it doesn't hurt to have a few extra prizes on hand in case of a tie. The following list will get you started:

- Fun note or message pads
- Stationery
- Mugs
- Candy
- Small potted plants
- Bottles of bubble bath
- Refrigerator magnets
- Novelty-shaped ice cube trays
- Coasters
- Recipe cards
- Kitchen gadgets
- Fancy soaps
- Hand lotion
- Guest towels
- Pretty paper napkins
- Six-pack of beer or bottle of wine
- Mixed nuts or snack foods
- Office supplies
- Golf tees
- Fishing lures
- Tennis balls
- Gift-wrapping
- Postage stamps
- Film
- Batteries

Serving the Food

Recipes

The keywords here are keep it simple. If you want to serve a full, sit-down meal (one that requires a knife), limit your guest list to the number of people you can seat comfortably at your dining room or kitchen table or at card tables. If there are rolls to be buttered or meat to be cut, and there isn't enough room at the tables, forget it! Asking guests to balance plates and cups on their laps (even with trays) is inviting disaster.

One way to get around the sit-down-meal problem is not to serve one. Instead, offer a variety of hors d'oeuvres, open-face sandwiches, and individual desserts. Serving these finger foods will:

- draw people to the table for snacking, thus encouraging conversation,
- keep conversations flowing and uninterrupted by a sit-down meal,
- permit guests to eat as much or little as they wish.

Consider these two factors when choosing your menu: what time of day the shower will occur and the number of people you'll be serving. The most popular times for showers are weekend afternoons and weekday evenings. Of these, only weekends at noon require a full meal. The others require only a variety of snacks and desserts. Large parties usually require a simple meal, even though you may want to serve a variety of fancy dishes. But trust us: You won't have time to fuss with intricate food preparations. Save those dainty canapés for smaller gatherings!

Lastly, consider choosing recipes that can be prepared before the party so you get out of the kitchen and into the fun. On that note, keep the beverages simple, too. You save lots of time by serving beverages that can be prepared in quantity, rather than serving those that are mixed by the glass.

And to keep you grounded, remember that regardless of the dishes you serve, food isn't the reason for the party.

Hors d'Oeuvres and Snacks

Tasty appetizers and snacks are favorite party foods, so there's no reason why they can't be enjoyed at showers, too. These foods are perfect for an evening or weekend afternoon party.

It's not hard to serve snacks that are tastier and more nutritious than chips and dips. In fact, you can serve a well-balanced meal consisting entirely of tidbits. Also include low-calorie foods, such as fresh vegetables, for those guests who are watching their diets.

Crab Hors d'Oeuvres

8-ounce package cream cheese, softened
2 tablespoons cream or half-and-half
1 teaspoon lemon juice
1 teaspoon Worcestershire sauce
Cocktail sauce
6-ounce can crabmeat, drained
Crackers or toast squares

In bowl, thin cream cheese with cream, lemon juice, and Worcestershire sauce. Spread mixture evenly on a plate. Spread thin layer of cocktail sauce over it, then sprinkle crabmeat on top. Chill. Serve with crackers and toast squares. Serves approximately 15.

Blue Cheese Nuggets

4 ounces blue cheese
1 tablespoon heavy cream
2 teaspoons brandy
2 tablespoons walnuts, coarsely ground
6 tablespoons wheat germ

Cream together cheese, cream, and brandy. Stir in walnuts and chill. Line baking sheet with waxed paper. Pour wheat germ into small saucer. Roll about 1 teaspoon cheese mixture into small balls. Roll each ball in wheat germ and place on baking sheet. Refrigerate at least 1 hour. (These freeze well.) Serve with toothpicks. Makes 40 nuggets.

Open-Face Shrimp Sandwiches

4½-ounce can deveined, broken shrimp
3 whole scallions, thinly sliced
3 tablespoons sour cream
4 tablespoons mayonnaise
6 tablespoons Parmesan cheese, finely grated
White pepper
14 slices party rye bread
14 whole shrimp, cleaned and cooked
14 tiny sprigs of fresh parsley or mint

Drain canned shrimp. Combine scallions, sour cream, mayonnaise, Parmesan cheese, and dash of white pepper with shrimp. Mix by hand until almost smooth. Spread each bread slice with 1 tablespoon shrimp mixture. Top each sandwich with whole shrimp and sprig of parsley or mint. Serve cold. Makes 14 sandwiches.

Spinach Dip

10-ounce package chopped spinach
1½ cups sour cream
1 cup mayonnaise
1 packet vegetable soup mix
8-ounce can water chestnuts, drained and chopped
3 chopped green onions or 2 teaspoons minced onions
1 loaf sourdough bread

Thaw spinach and squeeze out liquid. Add all remaining ingredients except bread to spinach and blend well. Cover and refrigerate at least 2 hours before serving. To serve, carve out center of bread loaf. Break carved-out bread piece into bite-size pieces and arrange them around loaf on tray. Stir dip thoroughly and pour into hollowed-out loaf. Dip can also be served with crackers. Serves 10–20.

Curried Egg and Artichoke Spread

6 eggs, hard-boiled, peeled
14-ounce can artichoke hearts, drained
¼ cup mayonnaise
½ cup sour cream
Salt and pepper
Curry powder

Chop hard-boiled eggs and artichoke hearts and pour into bowl. Add mayonnaise and sour cream. Add salt, pepper, and curry powder to taste. Spread on crackers or small rounds of cocktail rye. Serves 10–20.

Marshmallow Fruit Dip

3½ ounces marshmallow cream
1 tablespoon lemon juice
1 tablespoon orange juice
½ teaspoon orange or lemon peel, grated
¼ cup salad dressing

Mix all ingredients together and serve as dip for fresh fruit. Serves 8–10.

Artichoke Squares

Two 6-ounce jars marinated
   artichoke hearts
2 medium onions, chopped
1 clove garlic, crushed
4 eggs, beaten
½ cup bread crumbs
¼ teaspoon salt
½ teaspoon pepper
½ teaspoon oregano
½ teaspoon Tabasco sauce
8 ounces sharp cheddar
   cheese, shredded
2 tablespoons parsley,
   chopped
Parmesan cheese, grated
Paprika

Preheat oven to 325°F. Drain marinade from one jar of artichokes into skillet. Discard marinade in second jar. Chop artichokes and set aside. Sauté onions and garlic in marinade 5 minutes. Combine beaten eggs, crumbs, seasonings, cheddar cheese, and parsley with sautéed onions. Add artichokes. Pour into greased 8-by-8-inch pan. Bake 30 minutes or until set. Sprinkle with Parmesan cheese and paprika during last 5 minutes of baking. Cut into squares and serve. Serves 8–10.

Crescent Rolls with Gouda

1 package of 8 refrigerated crescent rolls
½ pound Gouda cheese
1 egg white, lightly beaten
Sesame seeds

Preheat oven to 325°F. Shape crescent roll dough in a star pattern on baking sheet. Place Gouda cheese in middle and wrap rolls around cheese. Pinch crescent rolls to plug any holes and brush top with egg white. Sprinkle sesame seeds over entire ball. Bake 15–20 minutes or until golden brown. Slice into wedges and serve warm. Serves 8–12.

Baked Mushrooms

8 mushroom caps, 1½ inch or longer in diameter
⅓ cup butter or margarine
2 tablespoons sherry
¼ teaspoon thyme
Salt and pepper to taste

Preheat oven to 325°F. Rinse and dry mushrooms, removing stems from caps. Place mushrooms upside down in shallow baking dish. In separate bowl, melt butter. Add sherry and thyme and bring to boil. Spoon liquid into caps until full. Sprinkle with salt and pepper. Bake 30–40 minutes or until tender. Serves 8.

Chinese Chicken Wings

1 cup water
1 cup soy sauce
1 cup brown or white sugar
¼ cup pineapple juice
¾ cup oil
1 teaspoon ginger
1 teaspoon garlic powder
20–24 chicken wings, cut in half

Preheat oven to 350°F. Mix all ingredients except chicken wings in blender or food processor. Pour mixture over chicken wings and marinate. Before baking wings, pour ½ cup marinade in jellyroll pan, reserving remaining marinade for basting. Place wings on top of marinade in pan. Bake 45–60 minutes. Brush with reserved marinade. Wings freeze well. Serves 12–15.

Sugared Grapes
Seedless red and/or green grapes
Granulated sugar
Egg whites

Wash grapes and separate them into bunches of 3–6 grapes. Lay bunches on paper towels to dry. Beat egg whites. Dip grapes into egg whites, then roll them in sugar. Set on waxed paper to dry. Refrigerate. Use to garnish plate of cold meats or other foods.

Other Ideas
- Wrap a slice of prosciutto around a wedge of kiwi fruit or melon.
- Remove pimientos from stuffed green olives and replace with smoked almonds.
- Boil small new potatoes. Dry them. Cut them in half and scoop the centers out of each, leaving a ¼-inch shell. Fill the cavities with sour cream and top with red or black caviar.
- Fry bacon strips until crisp but pliable. Wrap them around avocado slices brushed with lemon juice.
- Deviled eggs are good both as an appetizer and a garnish.

Luncheons and Brunches

A variety of foods lend themselves well to these meals. You can serve new, creative dishes, or simply serve your favorite standbys. Egg dishes, casseroles, sandwiches, fruit salads, poultry or seafood salads, and soups are all appropriate. Your favorite desserts are welcome, too, especially if you provide low-calorie options.

One easy, fun approach to an afternoon shower is a salad potluck. Guests bring their favorite salads or chopped salad ingredients. You provide a variety of dressings and rolls. Then simply arrange everything on a buffet and allow your guests to build their own salads.

Or consider preparing any of these recipes:

Impossible Quiche
12 slices bacon, fried and crumbled
1 cup Swiss cheese, shredded
4 eggs
2 cups milk
⅓ cup onion
½ cup premixed baking mix
Salt
Pepper

Preheat oven to 350°F. Put bacon and cheese in bottom of greased 9-inch pie pan. Blend remaining ingredients 1 minute and pour into pan. Bake 50–55 minutes. Let stand 5 minutes before serving. Serves 6–8.

Elegant Eggs
6 tablespoons butter
1 medium onion, thinly sliced
12 ounces mushrooms, thinly sliced
Two 6-ounce cans crabmeat, drained
4½-ounce can tiny shrimp, drained
8 eggs
1 cup sour cream
4 tablespoons dry sherry
⅛ teaspoon nutmeg
Salt and pepper, freshly ground
Paprika

Preheat oven to 350°F. In large skillet, melt 4 tablespoons butter over medium-low heat. Sauté onions and mushrooms until most mushroom juice has evaporated. Remove from heat. Add remaining 2 tablespoons butter. When butter melts, stir in crabmeat and shrimp, and toss gently until shellfish are coated with butter. Let mixture cool completely. In large mixing bowl, beat eggs well and add sour cream, sherry, nutmeg, salt, and pepper. Stir vigorously until well mixed. Pour egg mixture into skillet with seafood and stir to combine. Divide contents of skillet evenly between 2 greased 9-inch pie plates. Sprinkle dash of paprika over each. Bake 45–60 minutes or until toothpick inserted in center comes out clean. Let pies stand 10 minutes and cut into wedges. Serve immediately.

To premake, bake dish and let cool completely. Cover eggs and refrigerate 1 day. On shower date, preheat oven to 350°F. Let eggs warm to room temperature 30–45 minutes. Bake 20–30 minutes or until warmed through. Serves 8–10.

Cheese and Egg Brunch

6 slices bread, cubed
13½-ounce can mushrooms, drained
½ cup stuffed olives, sliced
¾ cup sharp cheddar cheese, grated
¾ cup Swiss cheese, grated
4 eggs, beaten
2 cups milk
½ teaspoon dry mustard
½ teaspoon salt

Preheat oven to 350°F. Place half of bread cubes in 3-quart casserole dish. On top of bread, layer mushrooms, olives, and cheese. Top with remaining bread cubes. Combine beaten eggs, milk, mustard, and salt. Pour over bread mixture. Refrigerate overnight. Bake uncovered 1 hour. Let stand 10 minutes before cutting. Serve with sausage, bacon, and breads. Serves 8.

Eggs Lorraine

16-ounce package sausage
2 tablespoons butter or margarine
2 cups cheddar cheese, grated
12 eggs, beaten
⅔ cup whipping cream
Salt and pepper, to taste

Preheat oven to 350°F. Brown sausage and drain. Chop into small pieces. Melt butter or margarine in 9-by-13-inch pan. Sprinkle half of sausage pieces on bottom of pan, then add half of cheese. In separate bowl, beat eggs with cream until frothy. Pour over sausage mixture. Top with remaining sausage and cheese. Bake uncovered 30 minutes. Serves 8–12.

Cream of Artichoke Soup
14-ounce can artichoke hearts, drained
10½-ounce can cream of chicken soup
2 cups milk
1 cup cream
2 cups chicken broth
Black pepper, freshly ground
1–2 bay leaves, if desired

Slice artichoke hearts crosswise. Mix all ingredients in saucepan, and heat just to boiling. Remove bay leaves before serving. Recipe can be premade and refrigerated. Reheat just before serving. Serves 6.

California Cream Soup
10½-ounce can cream of celery soup
10½-ounce can cream of chicken soup
⅔ cup light cream
2 cups milk
¾ teaspoon salt
⅛ teaspoon pepper
¾ cup avocado, chopped
¼ cup ripe olives, sliced
¼ cup pimiento, chopped

Mix soups, cream, milk, salt, and pepper in large saucepan. Simmer over low heat. Stir in remaining ingredients. Continue heating slowly for several minutes. Makes 7½ cups.

Zucchini Soup

1 medium onion, chopped	¼ cup dill weed
¼ cup butter	¼ cup basil
4 cups chicken broth	1½ cups light cream or half cream
12 cups zucchini, shredded	and half buttermilk
½ cup parsley, chopped	Salt and pepper, to taste

Sauté onion in butter until golden. Add broth, zucchini, and seasonings. Simmer about 25 minutes or until zucchini is tender. Cool. Purée in food processor or blender. Add cream, salt, and pepper. Chill at least 4 hours. Serves 12–14. Can also be served hot.

Parsley-Lettuce Soup

1 pound potatoes
1 medium onion, coarsely chopped
1 clove garlic, finely chopped
2 teaspoons fresh or ½ teaspoon dried tarragon
Salt and pepper to taste
3 cups chicken broth
    (or 2 cans chicken broth plus water to make 3 cups liquid)
½ cup dry white wine
½ head romaine lettuce, finely chopped
1 cup plus 2 tablespoons fresh parsley, finely chopped
4 ounces cream cheese, softened
1 cup heavy cream

Wash and peel potatoes and cut into chunks. In medium saucepan, combine potatoes, onion, garlic, tarragon, salt, pepper, chicken broth, and wine. Bring to boil, then lower heat and cover. Simmer until potatoes are tender (about 15–20 minutes). Halfway through cooking, add lettuce and 1 cup parsley. In blender or food processor, purée potato mixture with cream cheese until smooth. (Blend in 2–3 batches.) To serve soup cold, add cream. Refrigerate until chilled. Soup can be covered and stored in refrigerator for 1–2 days. To serve soup hot, refrigerate without adding cream. Cover and store for 1–2 days. Shortly before serving, reheat soup over medium-low heat. Add cream and reheat without letting soup boil. Sprinkle remaining 2 tablespoons of parsley over each portion as garnish. Serves 10–20.

Hot or Cold Green Pea Soup
1 small onion, quartered
2 medium potatoes, peeled and cut into eighths
5½ cups chicken broth
2–2½ pounds fresh peas, shelled or two 10-ounce packages frozen peas
½ teaspoon dried basil, crumbled
Salt and white pepper, freshly ground
¼ cup dry vermouth
6 tablespoons sour cream

Place onion and potatoes in large saucepan and add 4 cups chicken broth. Bring to boil. Lower heat, cover, and simmer 15 minutes or until potatoes are tender. Add peas, basil, salt, and pepper. Simmer 5–7 minutes. In food processor, blend mixture until smooth. (Blend in 2 batches.) Return puréed mixture to saucepan and add remaining chicken broth and vermouth. Stirring occasionally, reheat soup over low heat to let flavors blend about 15 minutes. Season to taste. If serving cold, let soup cool completely and refrigerate until chilled. Soup can be refrigerated for 2–3 days. If serving the soup hot, reheat it over medium-low heat until the soup is hot; do not boil. Stir occasionally. Serve cold or hot version with dollop of sour cream. Serves 6.

Broccoli Cheese Soup

2 tablespoons butter
1 medium onion, coarsely chopped
1 small clove garlic, halved
Two 10-ounce packages frozen broccoli
*   spears or chopped broccoli*
¼ teaspoon oregano
Salt and pepper
½ cup water
½ cup dry white wine
½ cup sharp cheddar cheese, grated
3½ cups chicken broth
¼–½ cup heavy cream

In large saucepan, melt butter over medium-low heat. Sauté onion and garlic until tender; do not brown. Add broccoli, oregano, salt, pepper, water, and wine. Bring to boil over high heat, separating broccoli with fork. Cover saucepan and reduce heat to simmer. Cook until broccoli is barely tender (about 5 minutes). Remove broccoli and cut into 2-inch pieces. Purée broccoli, saucepan contents, and cheese in blender. Return puréed mixture to saucepan and stir in chicken broth. Reheat over low heat about 15 minutes, stirring occasionally. Do not allow soup to boil.

Soup can be first stored at room temperature for 3–5 hours, or can be covered and refrigerated for 2–3 days. Before serving, reheat the soup over medium-low heat; do not boil. Stir in cream, season to taste. Serve immediately. Serves 6.

Cream Cheese, Blue Cheese, and Watercress Tea Sandwiches

½ bunch watercress
3-ounce package cream cheese, softened
2 ounces blue cheese
8 thin slices whole wheat bread

Wash and dry watercress, removing any tough stems. In small bowl, combine cheeses and stir to blend thoroughly. Cut off bread crusts and spread cheese mixture on 4 slices. Top cheese with 3–4 watercress sprigs. Top slices with remaining bread. Store in plastic wrap until just before serving. To serve, cut each sandwich into 4 triangles. Makes 16 sandwiches.

Dill Cream Cheese Squares

4 ounces cream cheese, softened
2 tablespoons fresh dill, finely chopped
16 small sprigs of fresh dill
4 very thin slices of rye bread, cut in fourths, or 16 small party rye slices

Combine cream cheese with dill. Refrigerate overnight to enhance flavor. Let the dill cream cheese warm to room temperature and spread on rye squares. Garnish with dill sprigs.

Open-Face Tarragon Chicken Sandwiches

8 slices firm-textured white bread, crusts removed
½ cup tarragon butter (recipe follows)
24 thin slices of chicken breast
Parsley, minced

Toast bread slices on 1 side only. Spread tarragon butter on nontoasted side of bread and arrange chicken slices on top. Sprinkle with parsley.

Tarragon Butter
¼ pound unsalted butter, softened
1 tablespoon dried tarragon, chopped, or 2 tablespoons fresh tarragon

In small bowl, cream butter until light and fluffy by mashing it against sides of bowl. Add tarragon and blend well.

Open-Face Danish Sandwiches
Dark pumpernickel bread, thinly sliced
Rye bread, thinly sliced
Unsalted butter
Smoked salmon, thinly sliced
Sardines, skin and bones removed
Canned baby asparagus spears, drained
Red onion, thinly sliced
Pepper, freshly ground
Lemon, thinly sliced
Small sprigs of fresh dill

Spread bread slices with thin layer of butter. Cover some with smoked salmon, others with drained sardines. Garnish salmon sandwiches with small lengths of asparagus, lemon slices, and fresh dill. Season sardine sandwiches with pepper, and garnish with sprigs of dill, onion, and lemon slices.

Prosciutto and Cream Cheese Squares
12 ounces cream cheese, softened
12 slices rye or pumpernickel bread
12 thin slices prosciutto
Black olives

Spread cream cheese on bread slices. Top each with folded prosciutto slice. Slice several black olives. Crown each sandwich with olive round. Makes 12 sandwiches.

Fantastic Chicken Salad
4 whole boneless chicken breasts
Garlic powder
Salt and pepper
2 tablespoons olive oil
2 tablespoons vinegar
2 tablespoons orange juice
1 head romaine lettuce, chopped
1 head iceberg lettuce, chopped
1 bunch spinach, torn
8-ounce package bean sprouts
4 ounces Swiss cheese, shredded
¼ cup fresh dill, chopped
3 avocados, peeled and quartered
6-ounce can ripe olives, pitted and drained
8-ounce can sliced water chestnuts, drained
4 eggs, hard-boiled and quartered
2½-ounce jar pimientos, sliced
1 red onion, sliced
Fresh mushrooms (optional)

Dressing: 1 pint mayonnaise
             ¼ cup chili sauce
             ¼ cup pickle relish
             2 tablespoons onion, grated

Preheat oven to 350°F. Season chicken with garlic powder, salt, and pepper. Bake about 30 minutes or until tender. Cut into large chunks. Marinate in oil, vinegar, and orange juice 24 hours in refrigerator. When ready to serve, combine remaining salad ingredients with chicken. Mix well. Combine dressing ingredients. Toss with salad. Serves 14.

Tropical Fruit Salad
20-ounce can pineapple chunks
11-ounce can mandarin oranges
8-ounce can green grapes, drained
1–2 bananas, peeled and sliced
1 avocado, peeled and sliced
½ cup sugar
1 tablespoon flour
1 egg, slightly beaten
¼ cup lemon juice
Lettuce leaves for garnish

Drain pineapple, oranges, and grapes, saving the juices separately. Combine drained fruits with bananas and avocado. Prepare dressing by combining sugar, flour, egg, lemon juice, and pineapple juice. If necessary, use reserved orange juice to make ¾ cup liquid. Mix well. Cook slowly, stirring constantly until mixture thickens. Cool. Mix dressing with salad fruits. Serve in lettuce-lined bowls. Serves 6–8.

Seven-Layer Lettuce Salad

1 head lettuce, torn
½ cup celery, diced
½ cup green pepper, diced
½ cup onion, diced
16-ounce package frozen peas, cooked, cooled, and drained
1 cup salad dressing (not mayonnaise)
2 teaspoons sugar
6 ounces American cheese, shredded
6 slices bacon, fried

Arrange first 5 ingredients in bowl. Spread salad dressing on top, making sure it touches edges of bowl to form seal. Sprinkle 2 teaspoons of sugar on salad dressing. Sprinkle cheese and crumble bacon on top. Cover tightly and refrigerate overnight. Toss and serve. Serves 10–12.

Honey Dressing

⅔ cup sugar
1 teaspoon dry mustard
1 teaspoon paprika
1 teaspoon celery seed
⅓ cup honey

5 tablespoons vinegar
1 tablespoon lemon juice
1 teaspoon onion, grated
¼ teaspoon salt
1 cup salad oil

Mix all ingredients except oil in blender. Gradually add oil. Drizzle over fresh fruit to serve. Makes 1 pint.

Fruit Salad in Melon Rings

11-ounce can mandarin oranges, drained
15-ounce can fruit cocktail, drained
20-ounce can crushed pineapple, drained
16-ounce jar maraschino cherries, chopped and drained
2 tablespoons strawberry or cherry Jell-O mix
1 cup colored miniature marshmallows
½ cup walnuts, chopped
1 cup (½ pint) whipped cream
1 tablespoon mayonnaise
3–4 melons (cantaloupe, honeydew, or both)

Combine all ingredients except melons. Chill until firm. Wash melons. Slice ends of melons to expose seeds. Scoop out seeds and pulp. Cut melons crosswise to form rings approximately 1-inch thick. Fill rings with fruit salad. Serves 15–20.

Desserts

If you're throwing an afternoon or evening shower, you can offer just dessert and coffee. Keep in mind your guests' preferences, though, when deciding between serving a sinfully rich, triple-chocolate, whipped-cream bar or a simple fresh-fruit plate. If you don't know guests' preferences, offer them a choice. And include at least one dessert not made with chocolate, since many pregnant and nursing women avoid chocolate.

Silver White Cake

For two 8-inch layers: 2⅛ cups flour, sifted
1⅛ cups sugar
3½ teaspoons baking powder
¾ teaspoon salt
½ cup soft shortening
1 cup milk
1½ teaspoons flavoring
4 egg whites

For two 9-inch layers: 2⅔ cups flour, sifted
1¾ cups sugar plus 2 tablespoons
4½ teaspoons baking powder
1 teaspoon salt
⅔ cup soft shortening
1¼ cups milk
2 teaspoons flavoring
5 egg whites

Preheat oven to 350°F. Sift flour, sugar, baking powder, and salt together. Add shortening. Pour little more than half of milk over mixture and add flavoring. Beat 2 minutes. Add remaining milk and egg whites. Beat 2 minutes. Generously grease and flour cake pans. Pour mixture into prepared pans. Bake 30–35 minutes or until done. Cool. Top with desired frosting, such as the one below.

Silver White Icing: *1 cup shortening (not butter)*
                                   2 tablespoons butter
                                   ¼ cup flour
                                   2 tablespoons milk
                                   2 egg whites
                                   1 teaspoon salt
                                   4 cups powdered sugar
                                   4 teaspoons flavoring (Almond is a tasty choice.)

Beat all ingredients together in large mixing bowl on high for 10 minutes. Frosting will be very stiff.

Frozen Lemon Delight

3 eggs, separated
½ cup sugar
Juice of 1 lemon
½ pint whipping cream
27 vanilla wafers
15–20 cupcake liners

Beat egg yolks, sugar, and lemon juice just until thick. Whip cream and fold into egg mixture. Beat egg whites until stiff and fold into mixture. Crush vanilla wafers and pour ¾ of crumbs in cupcake liners. Add lemon mixture. Sprinkle remaining crumbs on top. Freeze. Remove from freezer and refrigerate about 10 minutes before serving. Makes 15–20 servings.

Chocolate Peanut Butter Bars

2½ cups powdered sugar
2 cups graham cracker crumbs
1 cup peanut butter
1 cup margarine, melted
12-ounce package chocolate chips

Mix sugar and crumbs together with peanut butter. Add melted margarine and mix. Pat firmly in 9-by-13-inch pan. Melt chocolate chips and spread on top. Refrigerate until firm. Cut into bars. Makes one hundred 1-inch square bars.

Variation: Roll peanut butter mixture into balls and dip in melted chocolate. Refrigerate until firm.

German Chocolate Bars

14-ounce bag caramels
1 cup evaporated milk
18-ounce package German chocolate cake mix
¾ cup butter
1 cup chocolate chips
1 cup nuts

Preheat oven to 350°F. Combine caramels with ⅔ cup milk. Melt in double boiler over low heat or in microwave. In separate bowl, mix cake mix, butter, and remaining ⅓ cup milk. Press half of mixture into ungreased 9-by-13-inch pan. Bake 6 minutes. Remove from oven. Sprinkle with chocolate chips and nuts. Pour melted caramel mixture over nuts and chips. Top with remaining cake mixture. Bake 20 minutes. Cool completely before cutting. Keep refrigerated. Makes 50–75 bars.

Impossible Cheesecake

¾ cup milk
2 teaspoons almond flavoring
2 eggs
1 cup sugar
½ cup premixed baking mix
Two 8-ounce packages cream cheese, softened
Slivered almonds and crushed almonds

Preheat oven to 350°F. Blend milk, vanilla, eggs, sugar, and baking mix in blender on high 15 seconds. Cut cream cheese into ½-inch cubes. Add cream cheese to mixture. Blend on high 2 minutes. Pour mixture into greased 9-inch springform pan or muffin tin lined with foil cupcake liners. Bake until center is set (about 40–45 minutes). Cool then top with slivered almonds. Press crushed almonds into sides of cheesecake.

Sunshine Orange Cake

Batter: 18-ounce package yellow cake mix
          ½ cup oil
          4 eggs
          11-ounce can mandarin oranges with juice

Preheat oven to 350°F. Mix all ingredients. Beat 2 minutes. Bake 30–40 minutes. Serves 18–25.

Frosting: 8 ounces whipped topping
            3-ounce package instant vanilla pudding
            8-ounce can crushed pineapple with juice

Mix ingredients in bowl and spread on cooled cake. Keep refrigerated.

Bourbon-Soaked Chocolate Truffles

7 ounces semisweet baking chocolate
1 ounce unsweetened baking chocolate
4 tablespoons bourbon, whiskey, or dark Jamaican rum
1 stick (4 ounces) unsalted butter, cut into 1-inch pieces
2 tablespoons strong decaffeinated liquid coffee
6 ounces gingersnaps
½ cup unsweetened cocoa powder
¼ cup decaffeinated instant coffee crystals
Paper or foil candy liners

Break chocolate into small pieces and place in top half of double boiler along with bourbon, whiskey, or rum and liquid coffee. Cover and place over boiling water. Turn off heat. When chocolate is melted and smooth (approximately 5 minutes), beat in butter with electric mixer. Pulverize gingersnaps in blender and add them to chocolate mixture. Beat thoroughly. Chill mixture several hours.

Mix cocoa powder with instant coffee and spread on plate. With soup spoon or teaspoon (depending on size you want), scoop out chocolate mixture and form into balls. Roll balls in cocoa mixture and place in candy liners.

Refrigerate in covered container until serving. Truffles can be frozen or refrigerated for several weeks. Makes 20–40 pieces, depending on size. These are very rich, so you may want to make them small.

Iced Almonds

2 cups whole blanched almonds
1 cup sugar
4 tablespoons butter or margarine
1 teaspoon vanilla
Salt

Heat almonds, sugar, and butter in heavy skillet over medium heat. Stir constantly until almonds are toasted and sugar is golden brown (about 15 minutes). Stir in vanilla. Spread nuts on foil-covered baking sheet. Sprinkle with salt. Cool then break into chunks.

Phyllis's Raspberry Dessert

1 box vanilla wafers
½ cup butter
2 cups powdered sugar
2 eggs
1 cup chopped nuts
3-ounce package raspberry Jell-O
1 cup boiling water
2 packages frozen raspberries
2 cups whipping cream

Crush vanilla wafers. Sprinkle half of wafers in bottom of 9-by-13-inch pan. Soften butter and cream together with powdered sugar. Add eggs, one at a time. Spread mixture over crumbs. Sprinkle chopped nuts on top. Dissolve Jell-O in water. Add frozen raspberries and stir until they thaw. Cool. When Jell-O mixture thickens, spread over sugar-wafer mixture. Whip cream and spread over Jell-O mixture. Add remaining crumbs and refrigerate. Serves 18–25.

Turtles

Two 6-ounce packages pecan halves
1½ 14-ounce packages caramels

Frosting: *1 square sweetened chocolate*
               1 tablespoon butter
               ½ teaspoon vanilla
               1 cup powdered sugar
               2 tablespoons hot milk

Preheat oven to 325°F. Cluster pecans in threes on greased baking sheet. Put 1 caramel on each cluster. Bake until caramels soften (4–8 minutes). Flatten clusters with greased spatula or spoon. Cool slightly but frost while still warm. (This gives frosting a glazed look.)

For frosting, melt chocolate and butter. Add vanilla, powdered sugar, and hot milk. Add extra sugar for thicker frosting. Beat mixture with spoon until smooth.

Low-Calorie Desserts

Cheese and Fruit

A simple, nutritious alternative to a rich
dessert is a large round of soft or dessert
cheese, such as Camembert or Brie, placed
in the center of a platter and surrounded
by slices of crusty French bread, tasty
crackers, and slices of fresh fruit. (Apples
work particularly well and are available
year-round. Sprinkle apples with lemon juice to prevent browning.)

Watermelon Basket

An attractive way to serve fresh fruit is in a watermelon basket. Start by finding
out on which side the watermelon rests most sturdily. Before cutting, trace
the outline of the handle (making sure it's thick enough so that it won't wilt)
and the basket. The ridges of the basket sides can be straight, jagged, or
fluted, depending on your imagination and skill with a knife. Make the
basket large enough for fresh fruit, such as melon balls, seedless grapes,
pineapple chunks, kiwi slices, halved strawberries, and whatever fresh fruit
is in season. Decorate the basket exterior by sticking fruit, such as cherries,
strawberries, and pineapple, to it with toothpicks.

Date 'n' Nut Bars
2 cups chopped, pitted dates
1 cup chopped walnuts
1 cup whole wheat flour
¼ cup corn oil
1 tablespoon vanilla extract
¼ teaspoon salt
2 eggs, lightly beaten
16-ounce can of unsweetened, crushed pineapple, drained

Preheat oven to 350°F. Combine dates, walnuts, and flour, mixing well. In another bowl, combine remaining ingredients and mix well. Combine both mixtures in large bowl and mix thoroughly. Spoon dough into nonstick baking dish. Bake 30–35 minutes. Cool and cut into squares. Makes 36 bars.

Flavored Melon Balls
¼ cup unsweetened frozen apple juice concentrate, thawed
½ teaspoon ground anise seed
4 cups of assorted melon balls

Combine ingredients, mixing well. Chill before serving.

Pumpkin Pudding
15-ounce tub ricotta
2 cups mashed cooked pumpkin (or canned pumpkin)
3 tablespoons fructose
1 tablespoon ground cinnamon
1 teaspoon allspice
⅛ teaspoon mace
1½ tablespoons vanilla extract

Blend all ingredients in food processor until mixture is smooth. Chill then serve in sherbet dishes. Top with low-calorie whipped cream (recipe on next page).

Carob Mousse

½ cup carob powder, sifted
½ cup hot water
1½ teaspoons decaffeinated instant coffee crystals
3 large eggs, separated
2 tablespoons sugar
½ teaspoon vanilla
¼ teaspoon cream of tartar
3 tablespoons sugar
½ cup low-calorie whipped cream (recipe below)

Topping: ¼ cup blanched almond slivers
             ½ cup low-calorie whipped cream (recipe below)

Put carob in saucepan and slowly add hot water. Stir constantly until smooth. Bring to boil. Add coffee and boil 2 minutes. Remove from heat. Cool 10 minutes. In separate bowl, beat egg yolks, 2 tablespoons sugar, and vanilla until thickened. Blend in carob mix. In separate bowl, beat egg whites and cream of tartar until soft peaks form. Slowly add 3 tablespoons sugar and beat to stiff peaks. Fold whites and whipped cream into carob mix. Refrigerate 2 hours. Top with almonds and dollop of whipped cream. Serves 8–10.

Low-Calorie Whipped Cream

1 cup evaporated skim milk
1 packet unflavored gelatin
1 teaspoon fresh lemon juice

Dissolve gelatin in milk. Freeze mixture in mixing bowl until ice crystals begin to form. With chilled beaters, whip milk on high until it triples in volume, adding lemon juice at end of whipping.

Beverages

Because pregnant women should steer clear of alcohol and caffeine, it makes sense to serve beverages other than alcoholic punches and coffee.

When you're deciding whether to serve alcohol at your shower, consult with the mom-to-be. Ask her if she'd be comfortable drinking juice while the other guests drink wine or whether it's best to eliminate alcohol altogether.

Serving just decaffeinated coffee is probably a good idea—it's easier than serving both kinds and is more likely to please all the guests than serving only caffeinated blends.

June Punch

2 cups sugar
2 cups water
1 cup decaffeinated strong black tea
Three 6-ounce cans frozen lemonade, thawed
6-ounce can frozen orange juice, thawed
2½ cups (1 can) pineapple juice
1 cup fresh strawberries or one 8-ounce package frozen strawberries
½ gallon water
1 quart ginger ale

Make syrup by boiling sugar and water 10 minutes. Add tea and fruit juice concentrates. Chill 2–3 hours. Thaw frozen strawberries or cut up fresh strawberries. Reserve juice. Add strawberries, juice, water, and ginger ale to punch. Pour over ice in punch bowl. Makes approximately 1 gallon.

Raspberry Punch

1 can frozen raspberry juice concentrate, thawed
Lemon-lime soda or ginger ale
Frozen raspberries

Mix juice concentrate with water according to directions. Add same amount of lemon-lime soda or ginger ale as amount of water and mix. Float frozen raspberries in punch.

Firecracker Punch

4 cups cranberry juice
1½ cups sugar
4 cups pineapple juice
1 tablespoon almond extract
2 quarts ginger ale

Combine first 4 ingredients. Add ginger ale just before serving. Makes approximately 1 gallon.

Apple Cider Punch

1 quart apple cider
2 cups cranberry juice
1 cup orange juice
12-ounce can apricot nectar concentrate
1 cup sugar
2 sticks cinnamon

Combine all ingredients in saucepan and simmer 20 minutes. Garnish with orange slices decorated with cloves. Makes approximately 2 quarts.

Southern Comfort Punch

750-milliliter bottle Southern Comfort or 25 ounces Catawba juice
6-ounce can frozen orange juice concentrate, thawed
6-ounce can frozen lemonade concentrate, thawed
4–5 ounces lemon juice
3 quarts lemon-lime soda
Orange and lemon slices

Mix all ingredients and top with orange and lemon slices. Makes approximately 1 gallon.

Orange Blossom Punch

4-ounce jar maraschino cherries, drained
8-ounce can pineapple chunks, drained
750-milliliter bottle champagne
½ gallon orange juice

Fill 6-cup ring mold with water or juice. Add cherries and pineapple and freeze. Pour champagne and orange juice in punch bowl. Remove ice ring by dipping mold in 2 inches hot water then carefully flipping it over. Add ring to punch. Makes approximately 3 quarts.

Brandy Slush

2 cups sugar
9 cups water
2 cups brandy
12-ounce can frozen orange juice concentrate, thawed
12-ounce can frozen lemonade concentrate, thawed
Lemon-lime soda

Mix all ingredients together except lemon-lime soda and freeze at least 24 hours. Put dollop of slush in each glass then fill with lemon-lime soda. Makes approximately 3 quarts of slush.

Mimosa Punch

Mix 1 part champagne with 2 parts orange juice.

Fruited Champagne Punch

2 large fresh peaches
1 pint fresh strawberries
½ cup sugar
750-milliliter bottle Moselle wine
750-milliliter bottle Rhine wine, chilled
750-milliliter bottle champagne, chilled

Peel and slice peaches. Wash and hull strawberries. Place peaches and strawberries in large punch bowl. Prick fruit with fork in several places to absorb wine. Sprinkle with sugar. Pour Moselle wine over fruit. Let stand at room temperature 2 hours. Just before serving, pour chilled Rhine wine and champagne over fruit. Add ice ring, if desired. Makes 3 quarts.

Variation: For nonalcoholic punch, replace wine with 3 bottles sparkling Catawba juice.

Summer Sangria

1 cup sugar
1½ cups water
1 cup orange juice
½ cup brandy
1 large orange, peeled and quartered
1 lime, sliced
1 cup honeydew melon balls
750-milliliter bottle dry red or white wine, chilled, or 25 ounces Catawba juice

Combine sugar and water in large pitcher. Stir until sugar dissolves. Add orange juice, brandy, orange, lime, and honeydew melon. Let stand 2 hours. Add ice cubes and stir in chilled wine just before serving. Makes 2 quarts.

Note: Vary fruit according to what's in season and looks most colorful. Also, strawberries contrast nicely with white wine.

Serving Suggestions

- When serving large trays of small items on a buffet table, prepare two complete trays of each item. Then as the first tray on the table becomes depleted, the second can be brought out to replace it.
- Before pouring hot coffee or cold punch into a serving container, temper it with hot or cold water. Not only will this process lessen the chance of breaking a glass pitcher, but your beverages will also stay hot or cold for much longer.
- A basket with a handle makes a convenient and pretty bread basket. For an extra touch, tie ribbon around the handle and line the basket with ruffled cloth.
- Soups can be as plain or as fancy as you wish; they needn't be difficult to serve. Place a tureen on your table with a ladle and mugs. Set out a bowl of croutons for garnish.

Special Equipment

If you're planning a large affair, you may want to rent or borrow some of the following items:

- Card tables and folding chairs
- Coffeemaker
- Punch bowl and cups
- Pitchers
- Champagne glasses
- Large serving trays

Garnishes

A pretty garnish can add a festive touch to any serving tray or punch bowl. Here are a few ideas:

- Float an ice ring in a punch bowl or set it on a platter to keep appetizers cold. To make an ice ring, layer fruits, such as cherries or citrus slices, and water or punch one inch at a time in a ring mold. (By using punch instead of water, you avoid diluting the punch as the ice melts.) Freeze each layer before adding the next. Remove the ice ring by dipping it into two inches of hot water until the ring becomes loose then carefully flipping it over.
- Traditional garnishes are carrot curls, sculpted lemons, radish flowers, tomato roses, and scallion brushes. Refer to a cookbook and try to make them if you have time!
- Arrange a circle of shiny green lemon leaves around the edge of an hors d'oeuvres platter. Tuck in a few tiny mums, daisies, and small bunches of green grapes.

Other eye-appealing garnishes include:

- Cherry tomatoes
- Bunches of watercress
- Shiny olives
- Pimiento strips
- Avocado slices
- Lemon, lime, or orange slices
- Hard-boiled egg slices
- Cucumber slices
- Baby dill pickles
- Paprika (sprinkling)
- Crisp parsley or mint sprigs
- Crumbled cooked egg yolk

Buying the Gifts

Selecting the right gift can be fun. It can be a real headache, too, especially if you're not sure what the expectant parents need or want. Of course any new parents will appreciate gifts of clothing, linens, and equipment, no matter what their financial status. But don't hesitate to ask them what basics they already have, what color the nursery is, and so on. Be sure to pass this information on to the guests.

Practical Gifts

Here is a list of practical baby gift ideas. Less expensive items appear first, but keep in mind that brand names and sales can greatly vary the final price of any item.

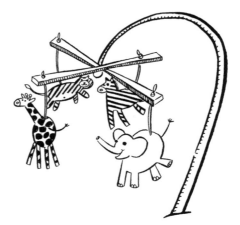

Clothing

Booties and socks
Undershirts (those that snap at the
    crotch stay tucked in better)
Plastic pants or fancy diaper pins
    (for parents planning to use
    cloth diapers)
Hats
Mittens
Hangers
Tights or hair ribbons
Sleepers
Shoes
Everyday outfits (babies grow
    fast—provide clothing in larger
    sizes, too.)
Special occasion outfits
Sweaters
Buntings
Coats

Nursery

Diapers
Disposable wipes
Diaper pail (liner refills are
    necessary with some brands)
Diaper stacker
Blankets
Waterproof pads
Crib toys

Mobile
Night-light or lamp
Stepstool
Changing table and pad or
    washable covers
Crib sheets, bumper pads,
    comforter, or dust ruffle
Crib mattress or waterproof
    mattress pad
Decorative items such as
    curtains, blinds, wall hangings,
    or wallpaper
Bassinet or cradle mattress or sheets
Dresser
Rocking chair

Meal Time

Bottles and nipples in a variety
    of sizes (liners are needed with
    some brands)
Insulated bottle wraps
Bottle brush
Dishwasher basket for bottles
Bibs (plastic and cloth)
Burp pads
Spillproof cups
Spoons
Divided plates
Nursing pillow
Breast pump

Booster seat
Highchair

Hygiene
Toothbrush and toothpaste
Shampoo or body wash
Baby detergent and laundry bag
Baby nail clippers
Brush and comb set
Bath thermometer
Bath toys
Tub-spout cover
Hooded bath towels
Washcloths
Bathtub sponge cushion
Bath ring (supports sitting baby
    in big tub)
Potty chair

Safety
Doorknob covers
Cabinet, drawer, or appliance latches
Outlet plugs
Furniture braces
Furniture corner cushions
Cord shorteners
Babysitter instruction book
Smoke detector
Monitor
Gates

Health
Cotton swabs or balls
Medicine dispenser
Thermometer
Nasal aspirator
Rubbing alcohol
Diaper-rash ointment
Ipecac syrup
Sunscreen
Acetaminophen
Teething ring
Child-care handbook
Medical record book
Humidifier

Travel
Snack cups with lids
Shades for car windows
Diaper bag
Car seat
Stroller
Infant carrier

Backpack
Portable crib

Play Time

Rattles
Balls
Books
Puzzles
Stacking or sorting toys
Musical toys
Push-pull toys
Ride-on toys
Activity centers for baby to sit in or
    lie under
Bouncing or vibrating seat
Swing
Toy box

Keepsake

Baby book
First-year baby calendar
Photo album
Birthday party planning book
Baby name book
Bank
Photo frames
Growth chart
Jewelry
Music box
Silver heirloom items
Starter savings account

Tip: Pile small gifts into a diaper bag, diaper pail, baby bathtub, or other large gift. The gifts could relate to the container. For example, fill a diaper bag with diapers, disposable wipes, air freshener, and other related goodies. Or fill a baby bathtub with a hooded towel, washcloths, baby soap, and a rubber ducky. Wrap small gifts individually to prolong the fun of opening them.

Big-Ticket Gifts

Often the most expensive baby items are the hardest for expectant parents to come by because they either can't afford them or can't afford the quality they'd like. Nevertheless, these pricey items are needed. One solution? Pool funds with guests to buy a big-ticket gift.

Furniture is often at the top of the big-ticket gift list. When shopping for furniture, check for sturdiness. Joints should have metal reinforcements at stress points. When considering a highchair, check how easily it operates. The trays on some models can be raised with one hand—a feature many parents really appreciate.

Or consider pooling funds to buy a matching ensemble of baby-related gifts. For example, buy a coordinating set of crib sheets, comforter, bumper pads, and diaper stacker. Check with the parents-to-be for preferences first. The gifts will be a bigger success if they don't have to be exchanged.

Handcrafted and Unusual Gifts

If these items are selected with the mom-to-be in mind, handcrafted and unusual gifts can be the hit of the shower, ones destined to become heirlooms. Making your gift gives it that personal touch that's sure to be highly appreciated. If you're buying your gift at a craft fair or boutique, know that the gift may not be returnable, so be sure it's in perfect condition—and perfect for its recipient—before you buy it. Here are some crafty gift ideas:

- Baby bonnet made from a lace handkerchief
- Bottle cozies
- Wall hangings
- Personalized puzzle or stepstool
- Personalized quilt
- Hand-knit sweaters
- Coins minted in the year of the baby's birth
- Embroidered training pants
- Fabric wall organizer with pockets
- Personalized porcelain baby bank
- Handmade cloth baby's book
- Fabric rattles
- Diaper covers
- Elegant baby basket
- Framed newspaper front page and horoscope from the baby's birthday

Gifts for Mom and Dad

If your budget can handle it, include a gift for the expectant parents. A pair of theater tickets, a bottle of champagne, and a certificate for an evening's baby-sitting can really boost overworked, overtired new parents. Here are some other gift ideas for Mom and Dad:

- Bubble bath
- Film or blank videotapes
- Disposable camera
- Frozen homemade meals
- Financial planning book
- Spa gift certificate
- Candy
- Gourmet coffee or tea
- CDs
- Fiction book
- Sexy pajamas

Gifts for Siblings

If the expectant parents have other children, consider giving the kids each a small gift, too. Siblings often feel left out as the family prepares for the birth of a new brother or sister. Giving big brothers and sisters gifts can help them feel included in the celebration—remember, their lives will also change when the new family member arrives. Here are some ideas for gifts for siblings:

- Quiet activities that can be done alone (coloring books and crayons, puzzles, and so on)
- Special afternoon or evening excursion (such as a trip to the zoo or park)
- Books
- CDs
- Stuffed toys
- Videotapes
- Clothes

Parenting Magazines

Expectant parents are likely reading about their baby's development and about parenthood. Help supplement their reading with a subscription to a magazine for parents. Below are some suggestions:

American Baby
This is a monthly magazine for expectant parents through parents of one-year-olds.
Phone: 800-678-1208
Web: www.americanbaby.com

FamilyFun
This magazine comes out ten times per year and publishes articles on crafts, travel, and leisure time for families with children between the ages of three and twelve.
Phone: 800-289-4849
Web: www.familyfun.com

Parents
This is a monthly magazine that provides parents of young children with general information on child rearing.
Phone: 800-727-3682
Web: www.parents.com

Parenting
This magazine comes out ten times per year and provides parents with general information on child rearing.
Phone: 800-234-0847
Web: www.parenting.com

ParentLife

This is a Christian parenting magazine for parents of children under thirteen.
Phone: 800-458-2772
Web: www.lifeway.com

Sesame Street Parents

This newsletter comes out ten times per year and publishes articles on child development, education, health, safety, activities, and food.
Web: www.sesamestreet.com

TWINS Magazine

This magazine comes out six times per year and publishes articles with multiple-birth parenting needs in mind.
Phone: 888-55-TWINS
Web: www.twinsmagazine.com

WorkingMother

This magazine comes out ten times per year and is helpful to women who continue working while raising their children.
Phone: 800-627-0690
Web: www.workingmother.com

Good Deed Certificates

Some of the most meaningful and helpful gifts can't be bought—for example, the gift of time. Why not give the mom-to-be a booklet of good deed certificates that she can redeem when she really needs your help: after the baby is born. Knowing that she can count on your help could be her sanity saver.

Create your own certificate book or use the format on page 89. Design the certificates on colored paper and then fill them out. Keep in mind your expectant friend's special interests and needs. And be specific; for example, specify "three hours of baby-sitting" or "one afternoon of baby-sitting" rather than simply designating an ambiguous amount of baby-sitting time. Consider certificates for the following:

- Baby-sitting
- Meal preparation
- Housecleaning
- Parenting advice
- Cup of tea and a sympathetic ear
- Parenting classes
- Decorating services or supplies
- Grocery shopping trip
- Ride to the pediatrician

Gift-Wrapping

Buy some pretty paper, ribbon, and a ready-made bow. Use an inexpensive part of your gift to decorate the package. Wrap your main gift and tie the extra gift to the bow. For example, tie ribbon around a baby rattle and fasten the unusual bow to the package.

Colorful gift bags are fun, too. Fill a gift bag with colored tissue paper, place your gift inside, and tie your card to the handles.

Make a beautiful tissue paper flower to use for a bow. Cut six to eight layers of tissue paper into 8-by-5-inch rectangles. (Increase the size to make larger bows once you've mastered making the smaller ones.) Use tissue paper in colors that match your package. Accordion-fold the layers of tissue in one-inch folds, then trim them like this:

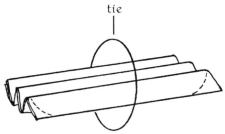

tie

Wrap a pipe cleaner around the center of the folded tissue paper and twist the ends together tightly to cinch the center. Fan out the accordion folds and gently pull out the layers to form "petals."

Tip: Ask guests to write short descriptions of their gifts on the backs of gift cards. This will minimize mix-ups and help the person recording the gifts. (Also see the Shower Gift Record on page 90.)

Appendix

Tips for Making Your Own Invitations

❧ Make sure you can find envelopes for customized invitations. You may want to select the envelopes first, then create invitations that will fit inside.

❧ To save money, create invitation postcards. Write party details on one side of the card, leaving room for mailing information on the other. Select a heavy cardstock so the invitations won't be damaged in the mail.

❧ Be sure to include all of the pertinent information on your invitations:
- ❑ Name(s) of the guest(s) of honor
- ❑ Date, time, and address (including directions) of the shower
- ❑ Your name, address, and telephone number
- ❑ RSVP information
- ❑ Theme information
- ❑ Gift registry information

❧ The way you address your invitations will indicate who's invited. If you're throwing a couple's shower, and you're inviting couples, include both partners' names on the envelope.

Baby Shower Clip Art

Add these baby-related designs to guests' nametags (without letting them see what they are) to play "Guess the Nametags" (See page 23.)

Diaper–Folding Illustration

For invitations, start with a fabric square or a paper square cut from a sheet of stationery. Write the party details (date, time, guest(s) of honor, address, telephone number) on it. Fold it as shown below and pin it with a gold pin. Be sure the diapers fit in the envelopes you've chosen.

  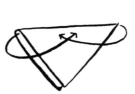

1. Begin with an open square of fabric or paper. Bring all four corners inward to meet at the center.

2. Bring the top point down to the bottom point.

3. Curve the right and left side points inward until their tips overlap, as in drawing 4.

4. Bring the bottom point up to overlap the other two points. Secure all three points together with a safety pin.

5. Finished diaper.

Teddy Bear Template

Use this template to make gift cards or nametags. Copy and cut out the bear.
Color it brown and back it with cardstock. Embellish it with ribbons,
buttons, and features drawn with markers.

Leaf Template

Glue a twig onto a large sheet of cardstock. Cut out leaves from autumn-colored sheets of construction paper. Write party details on the cutouts and glue one to each "branch" of the twig. Enclose in a padded envelope.

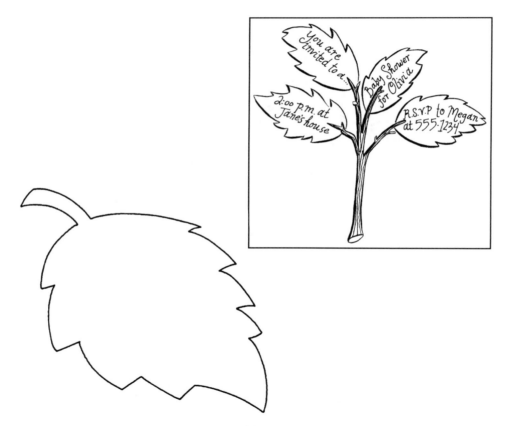

Cowboy Hat Template

Use this template to cut out cowboy hats from brown construction paper. Glue cutouts onto to the front of folded note cards. Embellish hats with ribbon for the hat band.

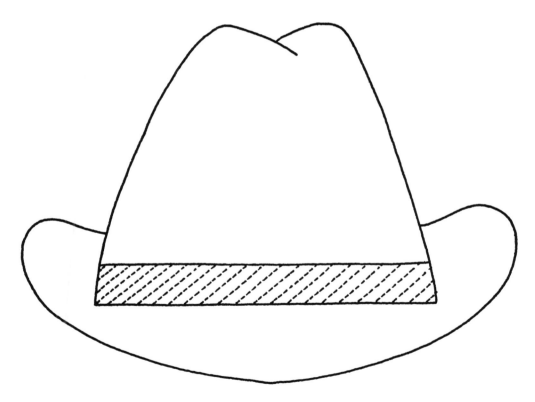

Baby Paper Chain

Accordion-fold a sheet of card-stock. The number of folds on the right side should equal the number of cutouts you desire. Trace a half-baby design onto the cardstock as shown here. Cut along the outline.

Unfold the cardstock to reveal baby paper chain. Write party details on the front and back sides of the chain and embellish the babies with yarn, fabric, and ribbon.

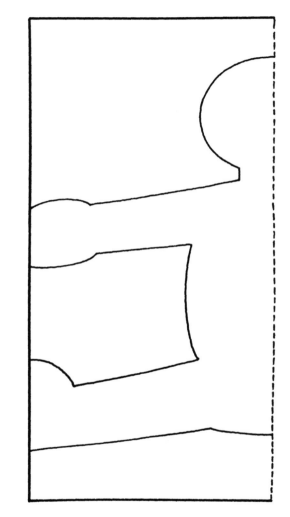

Sure-Fire Sex Determination Form

Ask the mom-to-be to answer and complete the following questions and tasks. Record and tally the responses on this form to determine if the baby's a boy or girl.

1. Tie a silver needle or a gold ring to thread. Hold it over the mother's belly. If the needle or ring spins, the baby's a girl. If it swings, the baby's a boy.
2. Lots of morning sickness? Then the baby's a boy.
3. How many cowlicks does the older sibling have? If the sibling has one cowlick, the baby's the same sex as the sibling. If the older child has more than one, the baby's the opposite sex.
4. If the baby's very active and kicks a lot, it's a boy.
5. If the mother's belly appears small for her stage of pregnancy, the baby's a girl.
6. If the mother's carrying the baby low, it's a boy.
7. If the mother's face has a soft, relaxed glow, the baby's a girl.
8. If the mother gained lots of weight early in her pregnancy, the baby's a girl.
9. If the mother's right eye and breast are enlarged, the baby's a boy.
10. Ask the mother to hold her head still and look to the right and to the left. Watch her eyes. If there is a red line from the iris to the outside corner of her left eye, the baby's a girl. If there's one on the right eye, it's a boy.
11. If the mother's sick during her first trimester, the baby's a girl. If her husband's sick during this time, the baby's a boy.

Baby Pool Forms

Copy and cut out these baby pool forms. (Be sure to provide enough forms for guests to bet more than once.) If you're collecting money for each bet, place the forms on a table next to a piggy bank with directions on how much it costs per bet and where the money will go. Be sure to mention the prize for the winner.

date of birth _____

time of birth _____

length _____ weight _____

sex _____

your name _____

Baby Pool

date of birth _____

time of birth _____

length _____ weight _____

sex _____

your name _____

Baby Pool

Good Deed Certificates

Copy as many of these certificates as you want, filling in the blanks with the useful services you can provide. Once you've filled them out, staple them in book form or punch holes in them and string them together with ribbon.

To: _____

For: _____

_____

From: _____

Good Deed Certificate

To: _____

For: _____

_____

From: _____

Good Deed Certificate

Shower Gift Record

Shower Date _____   Shower Given by _____

Guest   Gift Given

_____   _____

_____   _____

_____   _____

_____   _____

_____   _____

_____   _____

_____   _____

_____   _____

_____   _____

_____   _____

_____   _____

_____   _____

_____   _____

_____   _____

_____   _____

Baby Profile Form

As each guest arrives, choose a category below and ask him or her to give you an appropriate word to fill in the blank. Don't let your guests know what their suggestions are being used for. If necessary, create more categories and add them to the form.

Baby Profile

Date of party _____

First name _____

Middle name _____

height
_____

weight
_____

hair _____

eyes _____

male _____

female _____

occupation
_____

hobbies
_____
_____

favorite foods
_____
_____
_____

Also from Meadowbrook Press

✦ **The Best Baby Shower Party Games & Activities 1 & 2**
Each of these unique party game books contains eight entertaining games and activities, and each comes complete with tear-out duplicate game sheets for eight guests.

✦ **100,000+ Baby Names**
This complete baby-naming resource includes more names and more helpful features than any other book on the market. It presents over 100,000 popular and unique baby names along with origins and meanings, popular rankings, and icons denoting names shared by both genders. It's also packed with useful features like 600+ themed name lists and the latest naming trends.

✦ **First-Year Baby Care**
This leading baby-care book provides the most up-to-date medical facts to help guide parents through the critical first year of life with their child. It includes the latest newborn screening and vaccination schedules, updated reference guides to common illnesses, and expanded information on nutrition, including how to prevent food allergies and childhood obesity. Illustrations serve as visual tools to assist parents through each section.

We offer many more titles written to delight, inform, and entertain.
To browse our full selection of titles, visit our website at:

www.meadowbrookpress.com

For quantity discounts, call toll-free: 1-800-338-2232

Meadowbrook Press • 6110 Blue Circle Drive, Suite 237 • Minnetonka, MN • 55343